Mercury HeartLink
www.heartlink.com

Bruce Noll's Walt Whitman presentations have captivated audiences for over forty years; it is not surprising that his own poems bear the Whitmanesque earmarks of the close observations and reflections of a wise poet with an uncompromising eye for all aspects of life. The language through out the collection fulfills the insightful possibilities made in his *Fluency Joy*: "expression and body are one where words cascade in rhythmic synchronicity."

—David M. Parsons, 2011 Texas Poet Laureate

Bruce Noll's fine-tuned poems send a "sliver of iron/ across the empty air... to/ hear its pleasurable zing." His words nail down observations of the past and present, comb life's ditches for treasures, gift us with humor, humility, doubt, grief and tenderness. Noll so clearly reminds us of the earth in all its glories and disappointments, and what it means to be human.

—Twyla M. Hansen, Nebraska State Poet 2013-2018, co-author of *Dirt Songs: A Plains Duet*, Winner 2012 Nebraska Book Award; Finalist 2012 High Plains Book Award and 2012 WILLA Literary Award

Notes to
My Mortician

Street Sign, Granada Nicaragua

Notes to My Mortician

For Tracy —
my good friend
"Claim your own at
any hazzard" ...w.whitman

Bruce Noll

BRUCE NOLL

Notes to My Mortician
Copyright ©2014 Bruce Noll

ISBN: 978-1-940769-03-5
Publisher: Mercury HeartLink
Printed in the United States of America

Portrait photography by Hilary Noll
Cover art "Pyrops candelaria" ©Jo Whaley

Permission is granted to educators to create copies of individual poems for
classroom or workshop use.

Contact the author at: www.brucenoll.com

Contents

PASSING SIGNS

Song of the Nail	*1*
Part of a Script	*2*
Wood Showers	*3*
Harry's Voice	*4*
Lost Time	*5*
Laid Aside	*7*
Bum's Lunch	*8*
In Place	*9*
When Words Won't Come	*10*
Walking the Prairie Home	*11*
One Grandfather	*12*
Earthly Justice	*14*
Learning Country	*15*
You Boys Wait in the Car	*17*
Final Campaign	*18*
Left Behind	*19*

ENDLESS QUERIES

Self Exam	*23*
R$_x$	*24*
Schema	*25*
The Beginning	*26*

Absent Lament   27

If the First Word   28

In That Vineyard   29

Forward and Back   30

Quietude   31

Lost Words   32

Halter Call   33

The Poem Helpers   34

Pre-sight   36

No Candles, Please   37

The Nurse Asks   38

No Rose Colored Glass   39

Ferintillo Mummies   40

Notes to My Mortician   42

A Muse   44

LOVER LIVES

Feasting   49

Masonry Mixer Lover   51

Rising   52

Women to an Aging Man   54

Tea for Two   55

Not Really about Sex   56

Coming Back to Esther   58

Fossilized   60

Leg Poem #1   61
Swimming a Lake at Night   62
Warming Up   63
Set in Their Ways   65
So, You're Going to Potlatch?   66

LIVES ENTWINED

After the Party   71
Ben the Trucker Talks
    about His Mudflap Girls   73
Moves   74
Dave the Stone Mason Talks   75
1951 Minnewaukan County Fair   76
Neighbor X   79
Karl Talks by the Tractor   81
Karl Talks After a Hailstorm   82
Karl Opinionates on Interfering   83
Karl Talks about Cows   84
Oops, He Thought   85
Missed Mission   86
Enough to Turn Your Stomach   87
Unearned   89
Inside Business Meetings   90
Renewal Growth   92
Fluency Joy   93

OUTSIDE LIVES

Early Errors   97
Glass of Water   98
Killing Chickens   99
Journeyers   100
Spark   101
Bon Appétit   102
Uneasy about Certainty   103
Magnetic Confusion   105
Under Stones   106
Laika   107
Purposes   108

ABOUT THE AUTHOR   111

This collection would not have come
to light without the support and love
of Betsy, my lifelong companion.

I thank John C. Rezmerski and Paul Woodruff
for their keen critiquing of this manuscript.

PASSING SIGNS

Song of the Nail

Whitman never put the song
of a nail in his poems but
I'm betting he made some sing.

On long days, carpentering
with his father, unloading
wagons, hammering

square nails in fresh timber
the loafer in him would take over
and he'd savor the moment

of wood aroma, the warmth
of the sun, the handsaw's
"whisk-through, whisk-through"

rhythm between demands
of his father. I see him looking
at the sky, curling his big hand

to a slight arc with a nail nestled
across the base of his fingers.
Then with one swift wide fling

sending the sliver of iron
across the empty air just to
hear its pleasurable zing.

PART OF A SCRIPT

A writer is attempting
to put me in her novel,
to pattern my days,
hopes to sell me in the market.

She embellishes the thinness of
my character, makes me stronger than I am.
I become more complicated on the page,
more daring, more sensual and cast with
a tinge of sorrow, thanks to her.

In weak moments I'm tempted to give in,
let her dictate directions I might go.
In her fabricated adventure
I could face a challenging adversity
that might lead me to some tragic end.

Stubborn, no hero.
I've stuttered along okay so far,
still have lines of my own to say.

Wood Showers

Just great! I said.
*There's always something
I'm remembering too late.*

Just after I slipped
on the iced-over path
from the woodshed,
I realized the arm load of
split logs I'd flung to the air
needed to land somewhere.
They seemed to fall slower
than gravity's pull but swifter
than my hand to my head.

HARRY'S VOICE

Talking over the waxed string
of our oatmeal cylinder telephone,
Dad's voice, playful with serious tone,
hailed from Earth Central asking me,
Tom Corbet, Head Space Cadet,
if I had adequate fuel for my mission.
We pulled the sixty-foot cord taut between us;
I liked the feel of his tug on the line,
his childlike tones echoing in my oat box,
his complete attention to me.

In a pulpit his voice sang sonorous,
on the street, nonjudgmental and jovial,
at home higher pitched, tenuous.
Decades rolled.
Two days from death
Harry broke dementia's grip,
six hours distant from me:
Bruce! Is that you…?
was all that came,
not even "over and out."

LOST TIME

Beams of the father we knew
would stream through the fog and signal
the old presence we longed for,
and it seemed he would be with us
again for a time.
Moments of lucidity appeared in
those final months of Alzheimer mist.

On one of my last visits he sat in his
blue chair in front of the television
tuned to a golf game.
That's the one thing that he can watch for hours,
my mother said with hope.
He still makes some connection to that.

I sat with him and followed the players
on the course, all of us living out dreams.
Who's leading, Dad? I asked.
Where is this taking place?

I can't tell exactly. His voice was vacant,
as if he was thinking of something else
he wanted to say.
They don't play the way we used to do.
They'll play one hole and then jump
to another out of order. They don't
follow the numbers the way we did.

I hesitated.
Would he understand an explanation

about instant replay and tape delay,
or why the announcer would say,
Let's go back to number four a few
moments ago ... here's Els on seven
... back to Jim Furyk on thirteen?

I became the one befuddled.
Had he escaped his isolation,
making one of his old wry jokes?
If I explained the technological reordering
of time and events of the world
would I insult or belittle?
I fell into his silence, not knowing what to say.
We sat together then and watched the men
walk the fairways and greens with numbers
scrambled out of order on the flags.

LAID ASIDE

Some called
the death untimely,
which gave the widow
unsettled sleep but a few
years from their retirement
in a new house on the forest edge.
He left a nice woodshop—
drill press, table saw,
lathe and a wall of well
organized tools.

An aluminum canoe lies
bottom up in the trees.
A few rolls of sheep fence
are clotted with weeds.
The long wood pile has a tarp.

Plans wait still
in a pallet of concrete,
promise lives
in the compost heap.
Stories sleep in this man's books

and over there brush is cleared,
the beginning of a trail to the woods.

BUM'S LUNCH

An occasional hobo
would come by the parsonage
to ask for a plate of food,
which my mother would
always give.

I never asked if those
out-of-luck men ever
brought back thoughts
of her father who'd taken
to drink and was lost to her
many years before
he died on some stretch
of railroad track.

The stranger would sit
on the back step and wait.
Some took their time eating,
enjoying the small feast
of a sandwich and leftovers.
All were polite but Mom
kept us kids in the house.
When they left, she poured
boiling water over their
plate, cup and fork.

In Place

And the great horned owl
calls in the hollow

from the window
awakened I see the moon

on a westward decline behind
the winter skeleton of the hackberry

in the cattail thicket
across the meadow of snow

the ears of the cottontail
are as still as ice, still

as the field mouse burrowed
in its tunnels of grass

beneath the drifts, still
as this crystalline gift of silence.

When Words Won't Come

Don't come to me with complaint
of words that are hard to say.
I've had more than my share of
humiliation, of eating crow
when I wanted shrimp linguini.
I know about not being able
to spit out thoughts,
to make myself clear
or be quick witted enough.
You think you get choked
on phrases or find yourself
at a loss for words?
I know the true meaning of
dumb in dumbfounded.
There have been times
I could not bring myself to
utter a little, "I'm sorry,"
let alone to ask how to get
to Poughkeepsie.

WALKING THE PRAIRIE HOME

Our shadows extended
to long thin sticks on the
dust-filled road as we two
kicked stones, threw some
at fence posts, still others
at birds high on wires.
Late summer hum
and trickle of crickets,
the clack and whirl
of aging grasshoppers
and meadowlark songs
sweetened the air.
Crunch of PF Flyers on gravel
mixed with boys' boasts, challenges.

The clouds, waiting on the west horizon
for the drooping sun promised another
glorious sunset we'd take for granted.
Still another mile or more from home,
hot and thirsty in carefree trudge,
we toted our prizes left by farm workers:
two empty bottles of Hine's and Coke.
Then Kenny spotted the sparkle
of a Hudson hubcap in the weeds;
"May be worth 85 cents!" he said.
We spent a long time then,
combing the ditches without
a thought of how late
we'd be for supper again.

ONE GRANDFATHER

In the end
he was a rider of trains,
falling between tracks
into a thunderous night
of freight car wheels,
a bottle of rye
mashed on his hip.

They riddled his identity
from a police blotter.
A tattoo left on his arm
gave him away: four letters,
E-L-L-Y, my mother,
his eldest daughter.

No word had been heard
from William R. for twenty-six years,
this father of two girls and a son.
Once a modicum of joy in
lives of decades past,
anguish was his sole legacy
that snaked its way to us,
whispered and masked
like steam engine hiss.

Will's betrayal echoes
down the family line.
I hear him moan in late
calls of trains as they scream
across dark rails

approaching a grade crossing,
two longs, a short, one long,
asking tortuous questions.

EARTHLY JUSTICE

Before dust
it's soup we turn to.
In nature's last event for us
we simply bloat to become
a feast for flesh and blowfly
maggot puffs that sip
our juice of benediction.

The cold fact
and meat of the matter,
beetles like food dried
and consume our thoughts
through slow clean chews,
getting under our skin
and skinning us thin until
they desert our final spread
of teeth and bones

which then bleach
and are inherited by earth.
Our ultimate worth balances
out on the scales—
a gift to nematodes
and tiny bugs in dirt.

LEARNING COUNTRY

At first I loved the way spring breezes
splayed patterns of the yellow flowers
across my newly-owned hillside pasture,
gold interspersed among the emerald
tones of brome and old alfalfa growth.
And here and there, bull-thistles
poked up with bristled stalks and purple heads
where gold finches would later find a feast of seeds.
I was lucky to have bought a piece of heaven.

In a couple of weeks Lyle, a neighbor
a mile west who ran cattle across my north fence,
came by to troll our mutual border of
barbed wire and see what my wife and I
were up to on our fifteen acres.
As I rambled on about plans to build a house
and where the garden and pond someday would go,
he raised his foot to clamp down the top half of a thistle
then kicked the life out of the stem with the other boot.
I followed suit, glad to know the local technique
and to learn in a not so subtle way
that thistles were not flowers to farmers.

What you gonna do about the spurge? Lyle mumbled.

The what?

This shit here, he swung his boot
like a scythe across some small yellow blossoms
that tangled in his laces.

He went on to fill my silence.
It'll choke out your pasture, he said flatly,
..... and spread.

What do I do?

2-4 D is what most of us use.
Come over to the place and I'll give you some.
Get yourself a hand sprayer.
You've got a hell of a spell of work.

YOU BOYS WAIT IN THE CAR,

a command from Dad with
which we were glad to comply,
happy to be left alone in our
new red '49 Ford outside the store.
My older brother, Kenn,
had assigned me to my permanent
place in the back seat leaving
him free to explore the manual
in the glove box and
gadgets on the dash.

The cigarette lighter caught his eye
and he pushed it in. We waited in
silence for it to pop and at the *bing*
he pulled it out, looked at the spiral glow,
held it up to his cheek to feel the heat,
misjudged the distance,
and branded his skin.

Kenn never was one to cry out.
He threw the lighter to the floor,
writhing from pain, suppressing a scream.
Even at age six I knew how stupid
his mistake had been and had the sense
to hold back a giggle and, later,
to never mention his ring of scar.

FINAL CAMPAIGN

My mother fought the
devil for my father's mind.
In those last five years
the thief of memory bled
away Dad's identity as he
seeped into an abyss
of blankness and solitude.
She saw herself disappear
in him a bit more each day
and prompted his fading brain
to preserve what they
had lived and been.

Left Behind

I was raised under threat
of being left behind—
at such an hour as you think not,
as the Book of Matthew said,
wherein believers would disappear
into thin air.
The proof hung in our house,
a painting of a farmer working
in a field with a pipe dropping
from his mouth as he looked aghast
at a pitchfork floating nearby
where his companion had just been.
The idea of rapture was a real possibility.

At age seven I came home from
school one spring afternoon to find my
father, mother and brother gone.
My calls echoed through the empty house
as I ran from room to room,
saw clothes on my parents' floor.
Then came the panic of the inevitable—
I knew it was too late to pray but
was thinking of giving it a chance
when our car pulled into the driveway.
God had pulled a trick just to
scare the shit out of me.
I decided I didn't like
that game called blind belief.

ENDLESS QUERIES

SELF EXAM

Because light takes time to travel,
when I see myself in my mirror
I'm looking at a younger man.
I remember him quite well
though he appears startled
to see how old I've grown
and what I have become.
The fellow leans forward,
glares in my eye and snarls,
So what the hell you been
doin' with yourself?

R~x~

My doctor tells me
I need to lose 18 pound of sadness,
that it's weighing on my heart
and will damage other organs.
She says that load of sorrow
I lug around is why I have slumped
shoulders and am down in the mouth
much of the time.
She has me taking a daily dose
of happiness placebos and
Snap-Out-Of-It pills.

SCHEMA

Truth, silent and patient as a seed
in a furrow waits, trusting rain will come.

Or not come. To fail germination
can be as profound as the earliest sprout,

as the egg abandoned in the nest,
the sapling washed from its mooring.

It is not what could have been
or might become but what is.

The rock lying on the forest floor for
a thousand seasons creates a difference;

ask the generations of centipedes,
beetles and ants if it is not so.

THE BEGINNING

The genesis
that drew Jesus
to the wilderness

had to have been
a struggle within,
perhaps confusion

or loneliness or
hunger for more
time to explore

the voices whispering
from the curls of wood
off the plane in his shop.

Something made him stop.

He was overwhelmed with
questions of purpose,
of infinite connections.

ABSENT LAMENT

For whom did
Eve grieve more—
Cain, her first born
or Abel, the first
human death?

The murder took
both of her sons.
Abel lay dead
in the field,
Cain vanished to
the land of Nod
into sleeplessness.

Not even one word
in all that myth
mentions Eve's
deluge of woe.

If the First Word

was *light*,
there was never
a thought before
in all that darkness,

not even *fear*.

In That Vineyard

Mother Theresa admitted
to a visitor not long before she died
that God had not spoken to her
for more than thirty years.
She went about her work,
praying one-way conversations,
allowing the infinite to find
voice through her hands,
believing she would not be
given more than she could manage.
I just wish He would not trust me
so much sometimes, she said.

Forward and Back

I was remembering next week
even as I looked forward to yesterday.
Ever notice how some days are
more fun than others to do over again?

Some people say this time-skipping
must be exhausting for me but
I am energized by it. For one thing
I know how things are going to turn out
and don't have to fret about loss or
be concerned with how much I gain.

I know there are people who live
in the past and others who meditate
to try and stay in the moment. I met
a fellow once who was always looking
to the future and planned his whole life away.

You wouldn't believe me if I told you
what happens next month. You'll just
have to wait and be surprised. And, man,
was that an eye-opener for you!

QUIETUDE

There is still enough
silence in the world to
go around, for everyone
to get their share.

Even the cricket knows
to be patient and has
the wisdom to cease
its chirp and listen.

LOST WORDS

I loaned my pen
then worried for
the words lost to me

as the ink poured
out someone else's
thought or items
for a shopping list.

What if that liquid
had been savoring
a line of poetry
which had been
escaping me
and now was gone?

I watched
the borrower jot
in margins of her book,
some inklings
that perhaps
were meant to be
the spelling
of that one great
thought of mine
which now
may never come.

Halter Call

I heard the whistle
from the gate of
the green pasture,

the yoke is easy,
they said,
come see the
bucket of oats,
they lured.

I could not be
reined in
by the promise
of better grass.

The horizon
beyond the hills
beckoned me

to view hidden
canyons and
wayside streams
and waters
still with solitude.

THE POEM HELPERS

Once people know you write
poems they start suggesting
things for you, poking around
a closet of ideas, telling you
what verses to wear. Something
cute about what happened
to a cousin of theirs or how
a squirrel chased a dog.
It could be some irony in a
news story or—and yes,
this will happen—
an unusual cloud formation over
a lake you both happened to see.

Beware.
Nod an assent, smile,
and stay silent.
The suggest-person will think
your mind is already into an ode
or sonnet and will leave you alone
with what they are sure are deep thoughts.
Stay calm.
One word and they will
take it as an invitation to help you
compose, sapping any slightest
potential, if ever there was one,
for even a good line.

Let that foisted inspiration
slide as you cross off

their help invasions;
don't bring it attention,
they will forget it sooner than you.
If you enter into a discussion they
are bound to ask you the next
time you meet how "our"
poem is coming along.

PRE-SIGHT

You hear
before you see—

the rapids beyond
the bend as you drift
the smooth stream,

the wind shivering
cottonwood leaves,

the step of the deer
in the shadows away
from the light
on the forest trail,

the distance in
the voice of your lover
that says something
is not right.

No Candles, Please

The sin eater of the town
wandered the streets,
alone as a leper would,
helpless and despised.
He was welcomed
where there was death
to eat the crust of bread
laid out upon the corpse's chest
and to drink a pint of ale.

Make no death cake for me.
Don't bring round a sin eater
either, though I am far from faultless—
no one needs my burdens to ingest.
Nor do I need a priest to plea
or plot a way for absolution.

But should you have a notion
to celebrate my passage,
feel free to pass about a pint or two
as you give a gentle thought for
the friend who's led the way for you.

THE NURSE ASKS

How is your pain today?
On a scale of one to ten,
ten being the worst you
have ever felt?

By worst do you mean
the second time I hit my thumb
in two days with a hammer,
or when my wife left me?
Worse than when the anesthetic
wore off from where the doctor
cut out hemorrhoids or that
pain-in-the-ass foreman I had
in the New York factory?

Help me out here, give me
some guidelines . . . worse pain
than when I hit my head on the
rocks or saw my daughter
break her arm or my son cut
open his eye on the edge of a table?
What about hearing that
someone I loved had died?

To what do you compare your pain?
On what scale can it be weighed?
Can you look it up in your charts?
When you draw blood, what level
of sadness fills the vial and
spills across your heart?

No Rose Colored Glass

A breeze in spring
was a mere portent of fall,
she could already see the
buds of leaves turn
crisp and drab in autumn.
The luck of a friend
meant someone had
taken a part of her
share of good fortune.
Ever so hard to slip
into the moment . . .
a symphony was a reminder
of the day she gave up the clarinet,
the sight of a puppy
dragged back her dead dog.
She was always finding reasons
why life was not fair.
Hope was unsatisfied hunger.
She failed to find
the lessons of surrender,
the harmony of waves celebrating
their end in spectacular spray.

FERINTILLO MUMMIES

In the mountains of Umbria
there are dead people on display
beneath a church. You pay
a small fee to walk among
them, some propped up
standing, some laid out.
A few priests—the privileged—
lie in caskets, their faces
and remnants just inches
from where you peer in at them.

The completeness of death
was cheated here, for all
has not turned to dust.
Their skin, their hair, intact,
some wear clothes from
two centuries ago.
One has his eyes open.
The killer of the town lawyer
has a broken neck from when
he was hanged,
his head slopes to once side
and rests on his shoulder.
He seems still to be in pain.

Dry air is needed to preserve
these corpses so only a sheet of glass
with open space above and below
separates us living from them.
It's possible to disobey the sign

and reach over the window and touch
the face of one sad fellow.
My wife did so as she asked,
*When will I ever get
 to touch a mummy again?*

It felt like old parchment that held
an unfinished story, she said.

NOTES TO MY MORTICIAN
(A Final Position Poem)

READ BEFORE RIGOR MORTIS SETS IN:
I slept better on my stomach and
insist you lay me out in that manner.
The ventral down position is comfortable
and stops me from snoring, something
I don't want to do in a cavern underground
when my sinus cavities are wide open.

Adjust my segments in the following fashion:
Put the head on a small pillow facing to my left.
It's okay for my face to be slanting downward.
Right arm gets bent at the elbow so it curls
around my skull encompassing the pillow.
The left arm is to be folded in by my side with
the radius and ulna under the humerus,
the left hand curled and snuggled under my chin.

My right leg should be straight, patella down,
with the sole of the foot facing upward.
Now, and this is important, take the left foot
and place the large to-market-toe and the next,
the piggy-that-stayed-home, on either side
of the right Achilles tendon.
(You will note this will cause the left knee
to bend slightly out away from the right leg.)
Take care not to allow the left hip bone to rise
above the level plane of the other—
in the last half of my life I was plagued with

frequent back pain and don't need that
to flare up where you are putting me.

This body enjoyed sleeping at night,
during the day, after first or second breakfast
or lunch. It rested well on grass under trees.
Please give it the courtesy of letting it
fall into dust the way it gave me such delight.
Let its vertebrae crumble down on the sternum,
the fifty-two foot bones sink into a heap.
So far as I can tell, this will be my longest nap.
Let me settle silent into my eternal love
of earth and sleep.

A Muse

On awakening
this morning
I checked,
as every day I do,
to see if I could
fog the mirror.

When the time
comes that that glass
stays clear,
I'll have
some heavy
reflecting to do.

LOVER LIVES

FEASTING

This is not one of those
love-filled poems you'll
hang on your wall
above your desk or dresser.
You may not even come back to it.
But you need to know—
I like the way you move in the kitchen.

You've said presentation
is half the art of cooking,
not meaning, I know, what I see
in your swift efficient strokes
whipping potatoes or cream,
your fingers peeling
avocados for a salad,
your arms lifting to strain noodles
or the way you casually toss
together a marinade concoction,
something you've never tried
but know will come out right.
I especially enjoy the way you
scoop hot cookies from the sheet
to the waxed paper on the counter.

Can you tell I love this dance?

Your sip of wine between
the snapping of green beans
to be steamed, and your stretch
across the stove to check

the chocolate sauce
that will later trickle
over ice cream pastry
makes the perfect recipe
to arouse my hunger.

Masonry Mixer Lover

thumb and finger
feel the rightness
of mortar and

the wet fluid
slip of sand;

the tip of the
tongue knows the
bite of lime.

Rising

My wife is in the yard
looking for peaches
for our breakfast
from the tree.
She carefully tests
each one with a slight
squeeze and twist to see if
it is ready to release itself
to her.

She stands barefoot in her
nightgown and leans with
slow grace to feel each
piece of fruit as when
ten weeks ago she caressed
each new rose on the bush.

The flesh of her leg
stretches onto the
short stone wall
and she glides to a
new height to continue
her tender touch
for the most ripened peach.

First one, then another,
yields to her touch.
She pauses to breathe in
their scent and seeing me
from where I have watched

from the window,
smiles and carries her
sweetness to the house.

WOMEN TO AN AGING MAN

So, it has come down to
gracious and benevolent smiles
from young goddesses who
make way for me
as I lower myself from
the steps of a train.

I can gaze without excuse,
not need a line to con
a way to look at them.
I have no strut to impress,
though I do tend
to pull my stomach in.

How innocent are some
with their flawless skin
that sparkles in the sun,
while others know
beneath their flowing hair
how to please the passing men

And then there are the seasoned,
the ones with laughter I understand.
We have lived lives similar somewhere.
They have a touch of swagger,
a steadiness of hand and eye and have,
too, come to love what age can bring.

TEA FOR TWO

Every day at the end of lunch
and supper my mother and father
would dismiss us from the table
and have their cups of tea together.

My mother usually got the Lipton
bag first. They talked as she
watched the color of the
brew and knew just when there
was enough life in the leaves
to lift them to the other cup.

Two tea bags a day for most
of their sixty years together,
their lives steeped in
swirled moments
of sugar and milk.

Not Really about Sex

Those conversations with me
came late for my parents,
and then were about themselves.
I was fully grown, married,
Dad in his mid sixties;
we were alone driving somewhere.

> *There's no doubt I've always*
> *loved your mother but I've just*
> *lost interest in . . . well, intimacy.*
> *She doesn't understand.*
> *Sometimes at night, asleep,*
> *I get hard, you know the way*
> *men do, and Mom notices,*
> *gets mad, accusatory,*
> *wondering who I am thinking about.*

Decades later, two years after he died
from under the long cloud of Alzheimer's
my mother reminisced in the
nursing home one afternoon.

> *I know there was always a part*
> *of him that would come alive,*
> *be with me in the present—*
> *sometimes a look or surprising*
> *response to a word or picture.*
> *One night he woke, aroused,*
> *and started kissing me,*
> *wanting me.*

I gave in.
In the morning he could
not even remember.

Coming Back to Esther

I keep coming back to her
like that swing that slammed
my stomach when I was five

the older boys had jumped
from the wooden seats and run
out to the barn and I was left

glad for my turn but misjudged
the backward sweep as my hands
grabbed the rope the momentum

of the wood caught me in the gut
and I reeled from pain and hid
by the bushes against the house

crying even as Esther came to
ask what was wrong and put her
hand of comfort to my shoulder

embarrassing me that someone
found me in tears I kicked back in
anger catching her leg with my foot

to hear her say *OK little boy I'll*
leave you alone and walked away
when what I wanted was

for her to stay I peeked to see
it was her to whom I would then
ever look to from afar with

adoration for she never spoke to
me again as her offer of a little love
was spurned by my humiliation

and for years I dreamed of this
beautiful older girl terrified to
speak to her but worshipping her

every move at church and socials
and that spring at the two room
school when Esther let the boys

launch her in the air at recess
from her end of the teeter-totter
as they counted one two three

and slammed their end of the
plank to the ground to watch
my angel fly to heaven and

back to earth where I looked away
from children's cheers to where
Esther would ever reside in dreams.

Fossilized

Over years
you have become
infused in me
and will be
part of my dust,
pressed one day into stone.

In a million millennia
perchance some sentient
being will pass on our portion
of earth and see
some rift in rock and
pause to feel the
speckles of gneiss
and sense the love
that once lived there.

Leg Poem #1

This little love poem
is about your patellae,
those lovely fulcrum caps
midway down your legs.
I admire them when
you're not looking, or maybe
you know from how I put
my hand on them so often
when we sit near.

These bones of oval protect your
stride, let you run and bend,
guide the hinge between your
tibias and femurs—
oh, don't let me get started
on those for therein lie
long rhapsodic odes!

The best thing about
your knees is the
independence they provide
and I cherish the choice
you've made to walk with me.

Swimming a Lake at Night

The pull of my arm across
calm water vibrates the stars.

The hair of my beard, chest and thighs
are caressed, soft as a lover's stocking;
I am adrift in the Milky Way.

The wetness of silk
murmurs in my ears;

I raise my head for breath
then plunge again to cosmic bliss

to be one with the air and water,
one with this dark mystery,
one with jettisoned light in the night.

Warming Up

I have fallen in love with the
second row, third place in,
violinist.

She has no idea I exist.

I bought season tickets
in the left orchestra section
to be close to her and always
am in my seat before she arrives.
She seems so self-contained,
speaks little to other
musicians and takes but a moment
to adjust her chair and music stand
before running her bow across
the strings to fuse her mind
to the instrument and then becomes
as lost to the world as she is
oblivious of me.

When the full orchestra is loosening,
warming the hall with sound, I can
still pick out her solitary strands.

Rarely she lifts her eyes but
once her gaze fell across
the filing-in crowd and caught my
staring for just an instant.
I froze, not daring the slightest nod
and then she looked beyond, up to

the mezzanine, then turned to acknowledge
something a companion to her left had said.

I should have taken my chance and smiled.

SET IN THEIR WAYS

In the front seat she
still sat in the middle
close to him.
You'd have thought
after forty years,
after eight or nine sedans
she'd have tired of
rearview mirrors
impairing her view.

Sometimes for a thrill
he would put some pep
into right hand corners—
he liked the feel of her
leaning into him and
the way she, as in
old times, would grasp
her hand to his thigh.

So, You're Going to Potlatch?

If you run into a guy named Doug
tell him I still have his book,
The Voice as Instrument, and
that I'll get it back before too long.

Should you meet a woman called
Sally tell her I'm sorry; she'll know
what you mean. Oh, and there's
this fellow—you can't miss him—
he's Irish and about six foot four
with red hair . . . tell him I still have
his jackknife from that time
we went night fishing.

Joanne may not remember but see
if the song "Sixteen Candles"
rings a bell when you tell her
you know me. Don't mention my
name if you come across
a big dude they call "Birch."

Someday, if he's still around,
Vernon can tell you, after
six or so beers, about the time
we got lost in the woods.

And, not that it's important,
but if you run into a woman, Jackie,
in the Wagon Wheel on 6th and Pine
and you find she's not with anyone
anymore, give me a call.

LIVES ENTWINED

AFTER THE PARTY

Did you get to speak with that
new woman who was there tonight?

Which one?

Which one! The one all the men were
fawning over…I saw you gawking.

I wasn't gawking. I was interested
in what she does.

Which is…?

She's a physician, well almost,
about to do her internship.

And her specialty is…?

Urology.

And all you guys were trying
to get her to talk shop, I suppose.

No! Well, Bob was, and we were just
listening. You know, according to research
there might be new signs that can
indicate cancer in men…

Uh-hum…..

Such as a slight speckled coloration
around the glans . . .

. . . and what is the glans?   I mean you are
suddenly knowledgeable now, aren't you?

Well, yeah, I learned a few new things
I didn't know before . . .

I bet. She sure seemed to enjoy an audience, too.

Ben the Trucker Talks about His Mudflap Girls

Those two women
been coast to coast with me
twenty times or more.
Still look pretty much new
'cause I treat them right.
When I wash my windshield
they get polished up, too.
Chrome is still my favorite,
Silver got hit from behind
when I drifted off and slipped
onto a graveled shoulder in Idaho.
Sure woke up fast!
You can see a little dent
just beneath her breast.

MOVES

We jet west from Miami to Denver
following the blood of a sunset.
Above the flood of red,
a crescent moon in magenta sky.

A Bach sonata in my headphones
coming through the wire
hooked into the armrest
separates me from a beautiful woman
reading an article in Vanity Fair.

Somewhere over Alabama the sky turns black;
the moon, a thin circle of cream, tags along.

The woman styled in blue jeans and blouse,
light woven jacket, puts aside her magazine,
studies her left hand fingering a new band,
engagement or wedding,
embedded with small diamonds.
She slips it off. It leaves not the slightest
indentation on the flesh of her finger.
She contemplates her bare hand,
pauses, then returns the golden halo
across her knuckles.

Her right hand covers the left as
she looks across me through the window
to darkness and moon and distance,
wondering, as all of us do,
about decisions and destinations.

DAVE THE STONE MASON TALKS

I've known stones
that leap into your mind
and before you know it
they are rough and nestled
in your hands and
you know the place
in the wall twenty miles
away where they are
destined to fit.

Those are the ones
that go gentle into
the bed of the truck.

1951 MINNEWAUKAN COUNTY FAIR

I

DUNK THE NIGGER!
THREE BALLS for 50 CENTS
read the big red lettered sign.
Fresh from autumn harvest,
North Dakota farm boys
lined up to pay.
The Black carney sat caged
in wire mesh above a tank of water
taunting the ball throwers
with a grin thirty feet away,
ninety-five years past emancipation.

II

They were native Lakota,
father and son, whose customs
were not well understood by
children and grandkids of
Scandinavian settlers.
The audience in the stands
quieted as the Minnewaukan sheriff
inspected a six inch block of wood
then handed it to the father in headdress
who centered it over the chest
of his buckskin shirt.
He stood statuesque twenty paces
from his son who aimed a pistol.
The gun exploded, bringing gasps

from the crowd as the old man
fell to the dirt. He was helped to his
feet while the sheriff inspected
the chunk of wood, testified
it held lead and waved it
to a cascade of cheers.

III

Thrill seekers clambered steps
high to the platform just below
the lip of the giant barrel,
heeding the barker's hurry-up calls.
The wooden walls erupted to the
sound of a Harley whose woman
rider twisted the throttle, enraging
the cycle and rumbling the chests
of the watchers peering down from above.
She let go the clutch, and shrieked around
the wall cutting horizontal slices of space,
scaling each circumference with a
roar and whirl in a thunderous blur of color.
Down below on the cavernous cask floor
emerged another biker who
kicked his mount to life and screamed
spirals up to the edge of prairie sky
to join his companion, barreling threats
inches from the dumbstruck faces at the rim.

IV

Minnewaukan is now all but gone.
A growing Devil's Lake laps across

its old main street,
the Fair Ground dust is forgotten
under mud and water-weeds
where sunfish graze.
No Blacks are dunked,
no Natives do stunts
and the motors that troll
for walleyes swing calm
wide circles above and
beyond the past.

NEIGHBOR X

My neighbor confessed
to me that he has been
abducted by aliens.

More than once.

I promised not to tell
but, hell, I won't give
his full name or say
he works at the
local savings and loan,
is vice president in fact,
and is secretary of the
local Rotary.

I value his trust.
Things like this could
get out, he said, and ruin
a person's reputation
or career. Most people
are skeptics about beings
from another planet,
or more probably, according
to Gene, are afraid
to face the truth.

Last year Gene's daughter
was homecoming queen
at one of the two high schools
in town. He said he knew

that would happen five years
ago because aliens had
told him it would be so.

I don't think I'm betraying
his confidence in me to
mention his vacation last year
was not, as he let on, to
Monterey. Those seashells
he brought back were from
another planet seashore
far away. Just where,
as you'd expect of him,
he's not at liberty to say.

KARL TALKS BY THE TRACTOR

We should have sold out
after the death of our son.
The few times I raised the
idea it was as if the grief
began all over again.
She was afraid of moving
on I guess. What if we
forget? she said.

So we stayed. And things
were never the way they'd been.
Her life turned into like
that half-filled corncrib
over there . . . you can almost
feel a winter wind blowing
through those empty slats.
Even thoughts of spring
don't want to come.

Karl Talks After a Hailstorm

You can only plant what
has a mind to be planted.
There's not a hell of a lot
you can do about the weather,
something bigger, Nature, Fate,
some people like to say God,
but that never worked for me.
It's been said farming takes faith.
I say it requires a good
dose of acceptance.

Farming is about like
raising kids, you do what
you can and the corn,
barley, daughters or sons
will have a will of their own
in the end. That's the way of it.
How would you want
it any different?

Karl Opinionates on Interfering

There's a lot of places in life
that's not your fishing hole.
Hell, everyone's got problems
and while you help where you think
you might do some good, it's just
as charitable to stay out of
other people's entanglements.

Take when Tom Haggleman took so
sick and had to be sent away to that
state retreat. A bunch of us neighbors
took care of his crops and the women
helped out with Bonnie and the kids.

But when Craig Summers started
to cultivate Bonnie's personal garden,
things got ugly real fast.
You could say the same with all these
meddling wars our country gets into.
My dad always said,
step careful in the pasture,
especially if its someone else's.

KARL TALKS ABOUT COWS

I learned dairy from my dad looking
after them cows when I was coming up:
every morning before the school bus,
every afternoon when I got home.
Maybe it was working for them—
feeding, milking, shoveling manure
as well as putting up silage in the fall
and bailing hay in the hot summer
that got in my blood. I kept on the tradition
after taking over the farm.
They've got seasons just like us and we
lived rhythm of cows day after day,
learning their cycles and trying to time
the calving to keep the production up.
We always had about thirty milkers
which kept a bull pretty happy
puttin' out heifers or vealers every ten months or so.
Sure we took the newborns away, how in hell
you gonna keep them mothers lactating?
Most of the old farms had a herd . . . kept the
family in milk and butter and paid for
a lot of clothes and shoes for the kids.
You got to where you loved the smell of milk and cows,
even cow plops were aroma in the bank.
Course the bovines got rotated out after 4-5 years
when they weren't producing their worth in time
and feed. A lot of those old gals ended up
on our dinner table.

Oops, He Thought

It was a quiet ride
from the party.
Finally she said,

I thought I had told
you not to say anything
about my sister.

He knew she knew she had.

But it doesn't . . .
he paused, knowing he had
caught himself in his own trap.
Remember to never begin a defense
with the word *but*, he reminded himself.

He began again,
mouthing his words with
deliberate care . . .
What I thought was, knowing
Brad and Jan don't know your
sister, that they could offer some
insight into . . .

Don't even go there, she said.
You're not helping yourself.

They stared at the silent
dark road, the white lines
pacing their distance to home.

MISSED MISSION

They had dreams
for the moon one day,

to careen around the
crater-faced old man
to land instead of
an Armstrong
and Buzz Aldrin
in the milky dust,

to stand there awhile
and ride the wide arching
orbit around and watch
their water-world
rise in a dawn

before they burned in
an explosion of oxygen,
White, Chafee and Grissom.

ENOUGH TO TURN YOUR STOMACH

I'd stopped in at Jim's Welding
to pick up a small job I'd dropped off
a few days before. Jim was sullen.
He went back to a bench and
brought out the welded bar for
my mower. Handed it over.
Just four eighty, he said.
I gave him a five. *Everything OK?*
He looked aside, down to the
oil-stained floor. *Hell no. Shelly died,*
you know the brown lab. We was out
hunting pheasant on Saturday,
got back, I fed her kibble, gave her water.

His voice took on anger.
You ever hear of stomach
twisting in a dog?
Nobody has but the vet says that's
what killed her... said you should
never over feed a tired hunting dog.
Now how in the hell you supposed
to know that? He called it "gastic
torsion" or some damn thing, says
the stomach can get bloated and if
the dog rolls over the stomach gets
twisted, blood flow gets knotted up.
Why in the fuck don't they warn
you if they know about this stuff?
I've never seen it in a hunting magazine,
in any dog book. Sure as hell no

vets ever mentioned it.
Shelly was the best trained hunter
I ever had, a natural. Now she's
gone and I'm treated like I should
have known better.

No way you should blame yourself
for something like this... like you say,
who's ever heard of such a thing?

That's it. If the bastards know, they
should warn a guy. Everybody
gives their dog food and water after
a good run. You should be told.

UNEARNED

James lived baseball.
He pitched Little League,
won a lot of games.
But a line drive came too quick,
caught him in the stomach
hot as a Roman Candle.
A few days in the hospital
let the bruise start to heal.
A diet of watered down milk,
soft bread and creamy
medicine was hard for a kid.

James skipped Sunday School that week
then made the error to be on the street
just before noon when Lance Huseth,
walking home, ridiculed him,
made light of his excuse for missing church
and punished with a fist to the gut,
rupturing the swollen wound.
James died within the day.
Today he'd have been sixty-five.

Old Lance is retired by a lake some place,
fishing from a boat, guzzling beer,
listening to a Sunday ballgame
that's all tied up in the eighth,
same starters on the mound,
two runners on, two men out,
the count three and two . . .

INSIDE BUSINESS MEETINGS

In meetings when people
pontificate beyond belief
I imagine how their skeletons will look
when all their flesh has been pared aside.
I see that woman who gestures with flair,
waving long finger bones in the air
after those perfect colored fingernails have fallen away.
In a few years the man whose eyelids droop
as he pretends to consider a proposal will have
but hollow sockets when his eyeballs turn to soup.

That colleague at the end of the table who
rattles out opinions will one day have no
diaphragm to push his useless breath
between his naked ribs.
The day for the naysayer will soon be here
when her jaw no longer wags and lies
unhinged upon some rotting silk.

I study the bone structures of these folks,
see beneath self-serious looks and behind
the animated pretentious smiles the grins
of missing teeth and loosened fillings.

I rest my chin upon my hand as I pretend
to be absorbed by someone's proposition,
my fingers touch my temple where there
too soon will be a hollow space.
I scratch my scull—I think it will be
a handsome one bared of skin and hair,

then scratch the flaps of an ear to blur away
the drone of conversation knowing that
no one will care what is said this morning.

Tongues will cease their wag,
thumbs no longer cradle pens.
Pelvises will be free of buttock weight
and the rows of discs of the woman who sits
so tall and elegant across the table will crumple
and no one ever see again the lovely flesh
about her neck. That Perrier she sips will trickle
down her clavicle and naked ribs and those
soon to be forgotten well shaped breasts.

At last business meetings become tolerable
and entertaining at best as the chatter of
pompousness chips away the hour.
With this look at the longer run of time
things fall into place,
like the dust that settles after a flutter of wind,
like the dust that settles all of us.

Renewal Growth

I trimmed the desert willow tree
today that had crept to cover the
stop sign on the corner of my lot.
I've warned him about this before,
that it's a violation of city code,
that streets are given right of way.
Just last spring I cut his limbs back
with the beak of my pincher shears,
good clean bites that let me feel
vibrations of a satisfying crunch as I
seared through his green flesh and bone.
You'd think he would have learned.

Plants are not alone in stubbornness.
I guess I've been down that road
myself and know the kick of spite
and the dare of venturing where I've
been told not to go. I've also had
my wings clipped a time or two and
grasp the fact that that willowy sapling
amputee is thinking already of ways
to sprout more sprigs and leaves.
That willow likes to fill, like me,
the empty gaps of who
and what we want to be.

Fluency Joy

To have syllables
in sync with thoughts,
to have ideas roll
off the tongue
and leap from the lips
in a fluidity of motion,
as a swimmer
slips into the liquid space
where breath and muscle
are meshed with the flow
of the stroke and kick
and twirl of the torso,
to glide unimpeded
buoyant and forward,
to where expression
and body are one
where words cascade
in rhythmic synchronicity.

OUTSIDE LIVES

EARLY ERRORS

Bees bumbled
over one another
in the mayonnaise jar
in the hands of the boy peering in.
They vowed sting-less forgiveness
to him for release.

He felt their words buzz,
tingling his fingers,
heard their pleas
through holes in the lid
but himself was held prisoner
by power and wonder.

With his nose to the glass
he stared down honey-combed eyes.
First thing in the morning,
he said, and set them
on the stand at his bedside.

The next day the boy
was the only one to awaken.

He walked through the dew
bearing his chalice of bees
to bury them
in the garden with grief.

GLASS OF WATER

There is that moment—
surfers know—
when a crest of wave
at the perfect time of day
shows the blue-green of the sea
as a translucent window
against the sun.

It's just a flash when
sometimes one can see
fish, riding inside the power
of the curve of surf,
looking out with wonder
from that thin
sheaf of their world.

KILLING CHICKENS

One should never kill chickens alone.
There is something in the taking off of heads
that lets them get into yours;
a questioning cocked look makes you
consider the worth and rightness of the task.

Have someone share in the bloodletting
as you skin, gut, quarter and freezer-bag the meat.
Talking keeps the birds from getting under your skin.
Gossip about the neighbors' cows or daughters,
tell jokes as your next victims huddle
frozen and silent in the thin wired pen.
Congratulate one another on your fast progress
as you grab again a set of yellow feet
from the flurry of dust, squawks and feathers.

Clutch another bird in your arms, get the claws
and wingtips tight between fingers of one hand,
slip the head between two nails on a stump
set for the purpose, pull back the body and
quick-slip the knife over the stretched neck.
Hold the throb and thrust of muscle a full
minute away from your boots while
life-blood spurts on the grass.
Chat on about how you need to harvest beans
from the garden or what time you need to leave
to get to the softball game but don't look
at the moving beak and open eyes
in the bucket of guts and flies.
And wait a day or two to barbeque.

JOURNEYERS

The little night singers
were in the trees, the garden.
We sat outside at a table
with candle light
when a moth and
brown chafer beetle
came, as ships misled
across a reef by a false
guide, and rattled their
wings to the flame.

A young katydid came
to one of us who brushed
it from her arm. It lay
crippled with one hind
leg and one antennae gone,

while we went on
and on with talk about
bigger issues in our world
and sipped away our wine.

SPARK

This chill of winter,
warmed by the silent red finch
on the peach tree branch.

Bon Appétit

My cat savors pink
tidbits of left-over rib-eye.

He purrs as he chews,
ingesting the moment.

Almost as good as
raw mouse, he thinks.

Uneasy about Certainty

The black and white feathered
flash of the startled magpie
flapping from the ditch to the near fencepost
alerted my attention to the weeds
down from the roadside gravel.
I paused my morning walk,

parted the plant growth
to see a fresh road-killed skunk.
Its pink and blue viscera bulging
upon the coarse white and black hair.
Other shades of red, too,
in tubes of organs, struck life color
from the sureness of death.

Hours earlier
I had attended a wedding,
themed in black and white,
tuxedos, bowties, pearls,
black gowns and high heels—
a yes or no occasion,
an I do or I don't affair,
no room for questions
or time for indecision.

It's either time to cross
the road or it isn't,
time to eat or
wait for breakfast.

I stood hesitating,
the magpie holding me
in the ebony eye
of its tilted head,
both of us wondering
what my next move would be.

MAGNETIC CONFUSION

The little Scotty dogs
that came in a matchbox
never liked to sniff one
another's butt, black on
white, white on black
their magnetic attraction
always spun them face to face.

A physicist explained to me
a magnetic force is part of
the element of magnetic field.
Magnetic field is evidence, he
went on to explain, that the
magnetic force exists.

My head twirls from
the conundrum.
I go back to my Scotties
and pose the question to them,
and they but spin a tail to reverse
themselves again as if they are in
cahoots with the physicist.

UNDER STONES

Left unturned
stones keep lids
on tiny universes
of ants, beetles, millipedes,
nematodes and other lives
that like space dark and cool,
away from marauders,
drying sun and bird beaks.

Theirs is a routine in tunnels,
of egg laying,
living harmoniously with others,
occasionally eating a neighbor

or just lying in wait
under a granite dome
of quartzite stars
for something fortunate
or tragic to crawl their way.

LAIKA

Laika circled
the planet
in Sputnik II,
was dead within
hours after launch.
Stress and temp
extremes were
too much for
man's best friend.
She made a point
for technology,
was but a pawn
in international
tensions.

In Siberian forests
close to the
Northern Lights,
wolves cried long,
marking despair
for the first off-world
death of an earthling.

Purposes

Nature evolved its own reasons,
keeping leaves on some trees
longer than others

and grasses to bow their heads
with seed at differing
times of the season

and minds to bend back in age
to yield to a contentment
with life again.

About the Author

Bruce Noll's life has always been filled with poetry. As a child he wrote rhymes and memorized other peoples' verses where he found music and fluency in the sound of words. Born in New York but raised in Minnesota and North Dakota, this son of preacher spent countless hours on the prairies, in woodlands and beside the Mississippi River. In his early twenties he discovered the magic of Whitman's *Leaves of Grass* which has had a steadying influence on his life, and in 1970 he created and performed a program, "PURE GRASS . . . an experience with Whitman's Leaves". Since then he has performed it in 27 states and five other countries.

Many of Noll's poems have appeared in journals, magazines and anthologies. He has one poetry chapbook, *The Gospel Edits (2010)* and is the co-editor (with J. Smith & G. Kritsky) of *American Entomologist* Poet's Guide to the Orders of Insects (2014).

Bruce lives in New Mexico. He and his wife have three children and nine grandchildren.

www.brucenoll.com

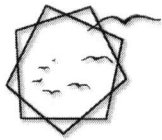